Men and Music

Isaiah Vianese

Coyote Creek Books | San José | California

ISBN: 978-0-9961824-9-2

Printed in the United States of America.

25 24 23 22 21 20 19 18 17 16   1 2 3 4 5 6

Published by Coyote Creek Books
www.coyotecreekbooks.com

for Alec Rigdon

Contents

Section II

I

Superstar

Mother's music taught me romance,
sitting on the dining room floor with her cassettes.

Those Saturday mornings, Karen Carpenter
hummed the weak, low tones

of hunger, frailty, the loneliness of being left
by a man for his guitar, the road.

Karen taught me about beds filling up in every town
with breasts, hands, navels, voices of different pitch—

taught me that each syllable was unique to those women
and foreign to her, to me, in a small town

listening and waiting for the love to start.

It Was Not Sex

It was the living room carpet,
six gin and tonics spread between us,
the skin that was yes, so soft,
the hair curled around my fingers,
mint-scented lips.
It was his shirt off, mine, and touch.
It was the way he said "Oh, your body,"
the way I said "I always wanted,"
but it was not sex—not this.
It was what could be held in cave of body,
in mouth, in gentle cave of hand,
the head thrown back,
the whiskered face littered with kisses,
but it was not sex. I want to be clear.
It was not sex at all,
but something we were making,
and what we continued to make
hours later, talking,
the rest of the town sleeping,
but us—his beautiful form dressed again,
his form pulled back from mine.

Men and Music

He loves popular music
so we sit in his car
sipping coffee,
listening to the radio.
He leans into me
as the music pulls,
pulls away from us
toward the blue night,
my hand on his chest,
his hand on my thigh.
Then he slips back.
The song has changed.

*

That night after the drag queen
sang my favorite song,
we went home, stripped off
the stench of smoke and beer,
the scent of men passing.
Above me on his handsome arms,
those eyes that lit the night,
I could still hear the song
playing, him breathing
those words into my mouth.

I Do Not Remember Much About Our Trip to India

Mostly, I remember standing naked
in the hotel bathtub, water
up to my ankles, washing his clothes,
wringing them tight against my body.

Sometimes he helped. Sometimes
he completed other tasks: wrote in his journal,
ordered room service (tea and French fries),
found something to watch on TV.

I did not know that I was already losing him.
Maybe it was the heat. Maybe it was the songs
repeating on our iPods—two different creatures—
or that we did not make love enough.

Maybe homophobes there and elsewhere—
we can always blame them.
I remember missing him.
I do not remember what happened after that.

A Sonnet to Confessionalism

Our first frost has come to pin us to this house,
this rusty hinge he calls our "domicile."
Sexton's been locked in an upstairs room all month,
cracking her ribs under some man's wheel,
while Plath tinkers with a corpse's bones in the basement.
She's always speaking German
and giving me some improper salute.

We've been too long in this ice cap of a town,
too long wishing we could mouth
some other emotion.
He says I speak too much of skunk hours,
dancing Mr. Bones,
but I say we must get out of here,
this headless horse of a home.

Drinking Song

Give me a body to hold tonight,
light, a sip, some song to sing

to bring him home again—

baby, put something bright to my lips,
if this tune calls you in.

Surrender

Walking home at night,
a man followed me for a long time.
Pulling the scarf to my face,

I hustled, worried
about my gait being too gentle
and wearing my tightest jeans.

He kept my pace,
flustered that I hurried,
the wind spitting darkness.

The street lamps seemed dim—
Matthew Shephard tied
to a fence again—

and I lamented moving to this city,
this wash of mini-malls
and frat houses.

Then he turned down another street,
maybe trailing me by accident,
maybe just giving up.

For Jamey Rodemeyer

Tonight, a pop star will sing
a tribute to Jamey, just fourteen
and dead by suicide.
Tomorrow, the news will have
a few words to say,
and his parents—those sweet,
heartbroken people—
will be given their chance too.
Months later, there will be other
matters to consider.
But now, a candle burns for Jamey
in a town not so far away.
Strangers are singing
his name like a prayer,
sending it up as a plea
to a god they hope will heed.

Winter Song

The neighbor's cherry tree
hangs low with snow.

While his father salts the step,
a young boy swings his shovel

up into the branches
to force the frozen weight free.

If Housman were here,
he might wish this boy

many springs to admire
the tree in flower, many Easters

fragrant with blossoms,
but one should wish the boy

many winters quiet as this,
the lasting kindness to love a tree,

even though it is gray with sleep.

Nocturne

Midwinter and out fetching wood,
I find the barn door frozen shut.

All is silent, the neighbor's dog
inside and resting on the sofa,

birds gone for months.
Smoke rising from the chimney,

the yard smells of pine,
and the houses on the street

are decorated with white lights
that look like stars.

I pull on the door again,
lean into it until the latch gives.

I gather a bundle to last the night,
dry logs that will turn to coal.

A Year is a Long Time

There have been other things:
the garden and its endless wanting, the old dog
asking for food, a walk, to pee in the yard.
I'm trying to say I haven't had a date in a while.

I haven't read so many books lately,
though I think about it.
I haven't written as much as I'd like to say.
I've made too many meals from a box.

My old boyfriend has someone new. He's settled down.
I mean I don't need things settled.
Someone could toss me up a little.
A year is a long time. I've done my share of longing.

Hummingbird

When we were in love
and lived together
my days were full with him,

but things fell out—as they
too often do—and he moves
further and further away.

On a walk, I saw
a hummingbird drink
from lilies in the park

and watched for a long while.
I knew there was sweeping to do,
the sink to scrub,

but I watched the bird
move from flower to flower.
Perhaps my love will come back

or he will not.
I will learn to live with that.
And the hummingbird—

his wings made him float
without a tether, without
a breath of wind.

A Song Plays

I slip back in time.
This flannel shirt gives way
to a black tee.
My hair shortens,
slicks to the side, 40s style,
and my jeans tighten
It's night.
Music from the bar
still rings in my ears.
A guy I will never quite love
has his hands in my pocket.
He tastes like peach margaritas,
and soon we'll find a dark corner
or a backseat.
When it's over,
he'll hum a pop song in my ear
and buy us two coffees with cream.
He will always send me home.
I don't know what will happen
in the years that follow—
the empty house and dark winters,
the joy that will eventually bloom.
I don't know how lost I've become
and won't learn for a while.

Still, I love the stars and warmth.
The guy nuzzles into my neck.
His hair smells of cigarettes.
I lean in to kiss him
but the song ends.

Fiona Apple Convinces Me I'm an Extraordinary Machine

You can only stay in bed so long
before the world bids *Get over it*.
For me, a winter of slumber
and a season of self-loathing.

Then you turn a corner.
I woke to a sudden summer.
The sun sat balmy over my house
and a breeze courted the window.

I turned on the TV, made coffee,
watched the grass grow,
and it happened. Not an epiphany,
but my feeling changed.

You could blame the singer
and her paper bag of a voice, or the heat.
Some new hope walked into the kitchen,
wrapped his arms around me,
and I knew I had made it through.

II

Joy

The night the singer signed my ticket,
I did not understand what she wrote
between my name and hers—
just three simple scribbles decked in stars.

Years later, I am dusting the apartment
while you and I chat on the phone.
Your workday has been long
and I don't like being alone.
We talk about our worries

when it becomes clear—
the word, "JOY,"
framed on the concert stub.
It had been there all along,
though it took me time to see it.

"Boyfriend," you say, "It's raining,"
then sing to a song on the radio.
You get drunk on the melody,
the chorus's sweet hook,
and I relish the timber of your voice.

"Teenage Dream" Karaoke

For our last week in the city of summer,
we spend nights bent over a bar,
savoring pints and popcorn.
This season, Katy Perry
is the number one singer on the continent.
Five, ten, fifty years from now
who knows if her name will be remembered,
maybe just a footnote
in a record book somewhere.

We may be forgotten too—
my black glasses, your cherry hair—
along with our friends,
this pub with a nautical bell,
and the city in which it lives.
But we dance in a room warm with light.
A local belts Perry's best tune
while we laugh and drink
like there is nothing better to do.

Crime

The only time I ever called the cops
I lived on Heartbreak Avenue.
A woman upstairs had a fight with her friend,
tossing glass and kitchenware.
For a while, I thought I could live with the crashing
but someone shouted, "Be careful of the children,"
and I knew what I had to do.

When the police arrived, they rescued
a boy not more than six and his baby sister.
I think of them, wherever they are,
and pray for their happiness.
It would have been a crime to leave them there,
just as it would have been
to let myself languish alone on that street.

Later and in another city, we pack.
Our attic room creaks, stripped of our things.
I sweat through my shirt
wiping every surface clean
and helping you load suitcases into the car.
I never dreamed of such joy,
a season warm with pleasure.

You and I delighted in this town,
our friends in every restaurant
singing musicals and gossiping about actresses.
Perhaps we will visit again.
The afternoon sun bakes the dashboard.
You turn up the radio
as I point our headlights for the hills.

Things Are Not Always as They Seem

The subway doors close tight like lips.
I lean into you
as the car passes from darkness to light,
sweating its way uptown.
I'm hungry. My feet hurt,
but I look at the photo we took
where a Haring sketch
is transposed across our chests.
You leaned in to kiss me
just as the camera snapped.

The train aches with the weight of passengers.
Some men sing the blues.
A woman shouts "the good news."
Tourists clutch playbills like gold.
I do not smile as much as I should
amidst this happy mess—
I mean, this happiness,
our thighs pressed together,
wandering minds at rest
as we clank our way home.

For Joni Mitchell

this morning on a street in Chelsea
clouds linger above condo complexes,
and traffic carries on with horns, squeaky brakes,
while men in suits call cabs,
women in black skirts carry coffee,
as the sun warms the city's face
and I remember your song
because everything is singing—even the wind,
even the man selling papers,
the garbage cans clanking, rank, and happy
with this morning on a street in Chelsea

I'm Into Pop Music

I'm into the river's dirty work,
coffee ground soot in a press,
perfecting the art of café au lait,
watching pigeons out a shop window.

I'm into Diane Keaton's thoughts
on Simone de Beauvoir,
the songs about too late and far away,
Carole King's affinity for mountains.

I'm into the biography of every woman
who was fearless and prolific,
poems by Edna St. Vincent Millay,
dreaming about music every night.

Can you see what I'm telling you?
Do you hear? I've got a lot work to do,
thoughts to have, things to say,
friends coming over for tea.

I'm interested in love.
Let's do some singing.

Yoga Song

The best teacher plays Top 40 radio
while she asks us to touch our toes
or reach for the ceiling.

I can't. I can't. Impossible.
My mind is a windstorm
and can upturn any pleasant room.

Thankfully, the instructor does not patronize.
"I love this song," she hums,
so I listen along.

A breeze moves through the studio.
I sweat. My legs shake,
but the air cools me—

a body imperfect but alive,
a heart doing its best to keep going.

Every Day a Holiday

We pass the gift back and forth every day
via phone and text message.
"Boyfriend, I miss you. You are the cutest."

Sometimes it arrives by mail:
a postcard from Kansas City that says, "I wish you were..."
or a pair of briefs and some music
to try while we are apart.

When we have sex,
it moves between us over and over
as you hold me up against the wall,
clench my hair in your hand,

or the times I want everything—
what did the singer call it? The river of stars?
Yes, then. When you offer me that constellation.

Beautiful

Your pants are loving my shirt,
their sleeves and legs entangled on the bedroom floor,
and my jockstrap is stuffed inside your boxers.

Our many socks are mismatched and kissing,
an orgy of cotton and polyester,
my clothes and yours wrapped into each other,
making one mass of sweaters and sweatpants,
my jeans with the copper buttons
holding your favorite hoody.

I like to think they are breathing there,
comfortable and cuddling.

I like to think this is how we live our lives—
separate pieces tossed together,
not always planned, but beautiful.

Hope

A friend washes her dishes
and looks out the window to see
a cardinal rest on a stop sign.
In a message she says,
"There must be a song in that."

This evening, the neighbor's dog
chases a squirrel in the garden.
He barks, knocking into lawn chairs,
but the rodent gets away.

Even with his ruckus,
I keep thinking about Katrina's red bird,
his melody
a shock of color set against the trees.

Whatever he sings about,
I'm sure it deserves praise, like my friend
who lives many states away
but is kind enough to write,
"Today, I saw this lovely sight.
I hope everything with you is fine."

As for the neighbor's dog:
he gets his own applause,
running after what he wants
even though he may never catch it.

Chinese Food

The streets are red lights on rain
as I walk home with our veggies and rice.
Here, happiness and despair live side by side.

See what you need to see—
candy-wrapper confetti,
bottles crushed into gems.

Water breaks petals free
from the Cherry Blossom trees.
Their pink sticks to my sneakers.

You know what makes me smile?
Those cat statues in Chinatown windows.
They always wave, each gold face grinning.

Work

"We all have work,"
I think, on my hands and knees
trying to get our bathroom tile clean.
The toothbrush I use is almost out of bristle,
but I keep scrubbing until the green floor shines.

In every building across town, people are busy:
waiters and waitresses polishing silverware,
market clerks bagging goods,
and gas station attendants checking ID's
before they sell six-packs and cigarettes.

Next door, the young couple who bought the place
spend all day unpacking boxes
and painting their windowsills yellow,
while the plumber moves
in and out with pipe and tools.

There is always something to get done
and tomorrow it will continue.
Rain will come and we'll track in mud,
as dishes pile in the sink
and the plants thirst for water.

So I kneel to my tasks,
a monk in the Church of Things-To-Do,
the detergent saints gathered
as I offer myself to this calling—
the labor of my life.

Nebraska, Sometimes

Sometimes I miss
those buttery afternoons,
a mystery on TV
and something sweet
crisping in the oven.
There was time
for reading at the cafe
and long walks.
When you came home from work,
we binged on burgers, fries,
and wine bought by the box.
We slept in,
made cinnamon buns,
watched too many movies.
The days seemed too common then,
but sometimes Nebraska
calls back to me
on a crowded subway
or when the fire trucks
keep circling our apartment building.
I think of how fat I grew
on its open spaces,
its creamy easiness.

Conesus Lake

Today my grandfather is fishing,
boat adrift on the lake,
his line baited and cast.
Years ago, he would have done this
between work days at the family grocery
where he was the butcher, carrying carcass
slung over his shoulder to the back room,
then separating meat from bone.
Now he works in an office
and can afford more time.
He will sit out on the water for hours,
craft bobbing, the fish biting and not biting.
Sometimes my brother or a cousin will go
with him to see what they can catch:
a pike with ragged teeth,
some sunfish—their bellies a creamy orange.
At dusk, he will return,
having freed all he has caught,
asking nothing of the world
and returning what he has been given.

Acknowledgements

Thank you to the editors of the following journals for first publishing poems from this collection, sometimes in earlier versions:

Assaracus: "Drinking Song," "It Was Not Sex," "Superstar," "Surrender," and "A Year is a Long Time"

Basilica Review: "Conesus Lake"

Door is a Jar Magazine: "A Song Plays"

Moon City Review 2011: "Hummingbird," "I Don't Remember Much about Our Trip to India," and "Winter Song"

nin: "Every Day a Holiday"

A Quiet Courage: "Nebraska, Sometimes"

Unfettered Verse: "A Sonnet to Confessionalism"

Wilde Magazine: "Beautiful"

I owe heaps of gratitude to my friends, teachers, and family for encouraging me while I worked on this collection.

"A Sonnet to Confessionalism" is for MaryJo Mahoney and Heather Bartlett

"Winter Song" is in memory of Jane Hoogestraat

"'Teenage Dream' Karaoke" is for Erin Francisco

"Yoga Song" is for Melanie Goodman

"Hope" is for Katrina Shilts

"Conesus Lake" is for Sherman Sanford

About the Author

Isaiah Vianese's poems and book reviews have appeared in *Assaracus, Blue Collar Review, The Fourth River, Lambda Literary, Moon City Review,* and *Rattle.* He is also author of the chapbook, *Stopping on the Old Highway* (Recycled Karma Press, 2009) and a book for children. He lives in New York City, where he teaches writing.

www.ingramcontent.com/pod-product-compliance
Lightning Source LLC
LaVergne TN
LVHW091233080426
835509LV00009B/1261